SEARCH AND RESCUE

Search and

Rescue

The Story of the Coastguard Service

NANCY MARTIN

DAVID & CHARLES
NEWTON ABBOT LONDON
NORTH POMFRET (VT) VANCOUVER

ISBN 0 7153 6501 0
Library of Congress Catalog Card Number 74-81053

Set in 12 on 14pt Times and printed in
Great Britain by Biddles Limited Guildford
for David & Charles (Holdings) Limited
South Devon House Newton Abbot Devon

Published in the United States of America
by David & Charles Inc North Pomfret
Vermont 05053 USA

Published in Canada by Douglas David &
Charles Limited 3645 McKechnie Drive
West Vancouver BC

Contents

Acknowledgements

I wish to express my gratitude to the following people who, by their courtesy and co-operation, have made this book possible:—

The Chief Inspector of Her Majesty's Coastguard and his staff, for their kindness in giving me access to reports and other relevant sources of information, and for providing facilities for visits to coastguard stations in Cornwall, Devon, Sussex and Kent

The many coastguards — regular and auxiliary — who permitted me to study their records and gave me a great deal of information about their work

The staff and students at the Coastguard Training School at Brixham who allowed me to sit in at their lectures and watch them cliff climbing and handling boats

The authorities and crews at Culdrose Naval Air Station and Manston Helicopter Coastguards and crews

The staff at North Foreland Post Office Radio Station

The authorities at the Royal National Life-boat Institution and at Trinity House, and

The authorities of the United States Coast Guard at the American Embassy in London; also the relevant authorities in Canada, Australia and New Zealand.

List of Illustrations

1
Smugglers and Preventive Men

On a dark moonless night in the middle of the 18th century a group of armed men gathered beneath the cliff at Birling Gap, near Eastbourne, on the south coast of England. They peered into the darkness hoping to catch a glimpse of an approaching boat. They listened for the sound of muffled oars making a gentle splash as the boat was pulled nearer and nearer the shore. It was their job to catch smugglers, and there were plenty of these around the Sussex and Kent coasts.

But the smugglers were crafty. They could afford to take their time. They knew the revenue men had to leave the shore when the tide came in. By the time the Customs men reached the top of the cliff the smuggled goods were landed and were being hauled up and carted away by confederates on the cliff-top. There were plenty of people willing to hide the kegs of spirits, the tea and tobacco, until it was safe to dispose of them. The contraband was concealed in wells, haystacks, cellars, under sleeping children and even in churches.

All round the coast, where there was any chance of landing their goods, bands of smugglers brought in tubs of spirits, coffee and tea from the East, silks and laces from France, sugar and spices from the West Indies and tobacco from America.

Customs duties were high and most people were poor and only too glad to be given a pound of tea, or a keg of

Smugglers bringing goods up from the beach

spirits for the risk they took. At Falmouth some tubs of spirits were hidden in a well and a haystack was built over them. Most people's sympathies were with the daring and courageous smugglers who risked being hanged, impressed into the navy or transported.

Smuggling had begun as far back as the reign of Edward I, when men known as *owlers* exported wool out of the country against the law of the land. Much later, when customs duties were charged on certain goods brought into the country, smuggling became the main occupation of those living near the coast, while New Forest ponies were used as packhorses to transport smuggled goods through the forest. There were few people living in the southern and south-east coastal areas who were not involved in the trade. Those who did not take an active part by bringing in and transporting the goods, either hid or purchased smuggled goods. People turned their backs to the smugglers as they passed through towns and villages so that they could say they had not seen them. Kipling was thinking of this when he wrote:

> *Five and twenty ponies*
> *Trotting through the dark —*
> *Brandy for the parson,*
> *Baccy for the clerk;*
> *Laces for a lady, letters for a spy*
> *And watch the wall, my darling,*
> *While the Gentlemen go by!*

When Customs officers did attempt to seize the contraband fierce fights broke out. There were killings on both sides but the smugglers generally had the best of it. The smuggling gang was usually the stronger party. Revenue men were poorly paid and were on watch for long hours at a stretch, so it was small wonder that very often they ran away rather than face the fierce onslaught of their attackers. Some accepted bribes and others were in league with the gang. When zealous Customs officials did succeed in bringing the offenders to court many magistrates were afraid to condemn them for fear of reprisals.

Smugglers had their own methods of avoiding detection. Sometimes, when hailed by a revenue cutter, they ditched their cargo in the sea and sailed back across the channel. But the goods that were ditched were not always lost. A hundred tubs were often slung together on a rope, with an anchor at each end to hold the sling on the sea bed. They were sunk with stones and marked with a buoy much as a fisherman sets his lobster pots. They

Revenue cutter Viper

could be recovered later with grappling tools.

One story concerns the notorious Hawkhurst gang. Their reprisals against those who thwarted them were so atrocious that they were feared by Customs officers and public alike. The people around Goudhurst, in Kent, were so alarmed by their terrorism that they formed themselves into a group known as the *Goudhurst Band of Militia*. Their object was to put an end to the atrocities. A retired army officer instructed them in the use of firearms and they made their plans.

The Hawkhurst gang heard about this. They sent a message to the Militia saying that, on a certain day, they would murder all the inhabitants of the town and then burn it to the ground. The Goudhurst people rose to the challenge. They were well trained and ready for the fight. After a fierce battle they beat off the smugglers, killing three and wounding others. Although this apparently drove the smugglers away from that particular locality, it did not stop them in their cruel deeds.

Shortly after this incident a Chichester man, who had joined the smugglers, was chased by a revenue cutter when he was sailing back from France with some brandy, rum and tea. For 6 hours the chase went on, with all sails set, until at last the revenue cutter fired some shots and the smugglers hove to. Their boat was captured complete with cargo, which was soon locked up in Poole Customs House.

That was only the beginning of the story. With the Hawkhurst gang to lead them, the smugglers broke open the Customs House and stole back the contraband. For a time they got away with it; then a reward was offered for information which would lead to their capture. They seized the informer and a Customs officer who was with him. The gang inflicted the most horrible and barbarous tortures on them before committting them to a dreadful death. After that everyone was even more in fear of these brutal men and they lost completely what remained of the public sympathy they had enjoyed for so long. Eventually the leaders were arrested and hanged.

Yet this did not deter the smugglers. On the contrary, they became more and more numerous and influential. By the end of the Napoleonic war in 1815, more than half the spirits which were imported were smuggled into the country without payment of duty. Something really drastic had to be done about it, and the Preventive Water Guard was formed. Large numbers of seamen were stationed along the coasts of Kent and Sussex, where most of the traffic took place. The smugglers retaliated by operating more

The Hawkhurst gang breaking into the Customs House at Poole

widely in other parts, and it become necessary to guard the whole coastline.

Until then there had been a number of different naval and revenue services working at sea and on shore, independently of each other. All had similar duties—the prevention of smuggling. These were the foundation of HM Coastguard, which came into being under that name in 1822.

At first it was controlled by the Board of Customs, but the Admiralty was responsible for the men employed as coastguards, who were all sea-faring men. From dusk until dawn, all through the year, the men were on watch at stations all round the coast. They were armed with pistols, cutlasses, muskets and bayonets. They needed these weapons for they were up against large bands of desperate men who fought pitched battles on the beaches and often succeeded in killing or driving off the coastguard while they landed their illicit cargo.

Gradually, however, the Coastguard began to win, and by 1856 smuggling was no longer a profitable occupation.

Besides dealing with smugglers, and having life-saving duties, HM Coastguard were members of the armed forces. Three thousand of their number took part in the Crimean War in 1854 and many more in World War I and World War II. In 1938, before the outbreak of World War II, volunteers were enrolled as auxiliary coastguards. They followed their own employment during the day and had regular training in coastguard duties in their spare time. This was the beginning of the auxiliary coastguard which forms the major part of the service today.

When war broke out in 1939 HM Coastguard became a war-watching organisation. Auxiliary coastguards shared with the regular officers the constant watch at the various coastal stations for the approach of enemy forces. They searched the coast for any suspicious incidents. They dealt with mines which were washed ashore, making them safe until they could be disposed of. Coastguards manned signal stations and did all shore wireless work. They recruited men from the navy and trained recruits in wireless telegraphy. It was not until 1945 that HM Coastguard ceased its connection with the armed forces.

Other countries also had their smuggling problems. In the latter part of the 18th century, when smuggling was at its height in England, America was fighting her own war against smugglers. They were robbing the country of so much money by evasion of taxes that the Treasury was almost empty. To overcome this the Revenue Marine, or Revenue Cutter Service, was founded on 4 August 1790. It started with ten cutters for the collection of revenue. These were fast boats, and when America declared war on England in 1812, six more cutters were added. They were engaged in chasing British privateers who were seizing American ships and impressing the seamen into the British Navy.

From its origin the United States Coast Guard was one of the country's armed forces. Unlike Great Britain it still retains this duty.

The Canadian Coast Guard was never an armed service so far as fighting was concerned, but for a period before World War I some Marine Service ships employed as fishing cruisers carried small guns which were used for naval training. Now no armament is carried and the Canadian Coast Guard is a civilian service with no military or police functions. It had been in existence as the Canadian Marine Service from 1867 until January 1962 when it adopted the name of Canadian Coast Guard.

Smuggling in America declined about the same time as it did in England, and then the Coast Guard was no longer employed in chasing smugglers. Its main objective was the saving of life through search and rescue.

The following chapters will show that the services of the coastguard are more needed today in all countries than they were in the old days of smuggling.

NOTE: Canada and the United States always use two words when writing about their Coast Guard. An individual in these services is known as a Coast Guardsman.

2
World Coastguard

HM Coastguard has always maintained strong links with coastguards in other countries. Marine search and rescue is an international commitment. There have been international meetings on the subject under the auspices of IMCO (International Maritime Consultative Organisation). Vessels of all nations can be found on the sea in all parts of the world. All ships have a very close link with the US Coast Guard through what is known as AMVER, which stands for Automated Merchant Vessel Report. Any ship can have a free call to the US Coast Guard if they are in trouble within 150 to 200 miles from the coast. In turn, HM Coastguard can contact America direct to enquire if a ship is in that area. Within a quarter of an hour the US Coast Guard can give a picture of the ship's new area.

While Britain has a separate organisation for different rescue and navigational services, the US Coast Guard operates them all: lighthouses and lightships, lifeboats,

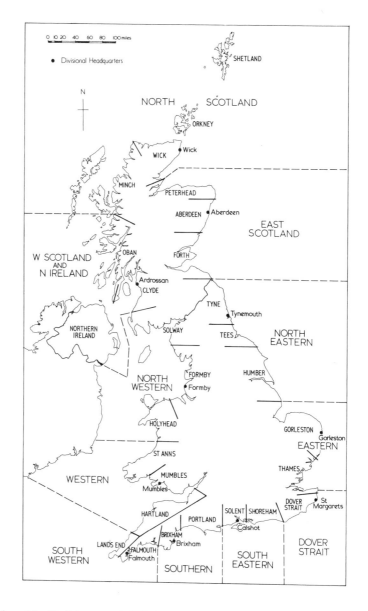

The 11 divisions of HM Coastguard around the British Isles and their headquarters

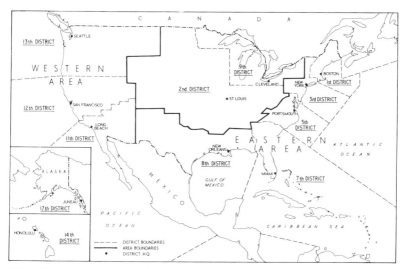

The US Coast Guard was composed of 17 districts during World War II, but after the war the responsibilities of several of the smaller areas were assigned to larger districts

pilotage, port security, merchant marine safety, fishing protection, law enforcement, oceanography and protection of seals. All these and many more tasks are the responsibility of the US Coast Guard.

Few people realise that the US Coast Guard has a headquarters at the American Embassy in London, employing a busy and sizeable staff. They keep in close contact with the Department of Trade and Industry, with HM Coastguard and with Trinity House. The US Coast Guard has more than 300 ships, besides helicopters and fixed-wing aircraft and shore units. It employs about 40,000 people, and with 10,000 miles of coastline to cover, and all kinds of navigational conditions, this large force is much needed.

The Canadian Coast Guard follows the American pattern almost exactly. It is operated by the Ministry of Transport, its business being to engage in ice-breaking, keep shipping channels safely marked and be responsible for search and rescue operations. It maintains and supplies shore-based and floating aids to navigation in Canadian waters, on rivers, the Great Lakes and other inland waters. Ice-breaking has always been an important role. For this purpose there are nine full ice-breaking ships and nine others which are light ice-breaking lighthouse and buoy tenders. Work in Arctic areas forms an important

US Coast Guard ice-breaker Eastwind *rides up on to a thick ice ledge and lets the weight of her fall break the ice*

part of Coast Guard activities. Besides giving primary ice-breaking support to shipping, numerous rescue missions are made to help fishing vessels in distress, either jammed by ice or requiring water-pumps to keep them afloat after sustaining damage. Other units engage in flood control, breaking up ice concentrations to avoid the risk of rivers overflowing their banks. Ice-breakers also go on mercy missions to remote regions such as Labrador to provide vital supplies.

Ice reconnaissance services are carried out by fixed-wing aircraft. Space satellites transmit photos which are successfully used in the assessment and forecasting of Arctic ice conditions. In 1969 a Coast Guard ship escorted the tanker which was the first industrial ship to pass through the Northwest Passage.

Coast Guard rescue officers are stationed at Co-ordination Centres. They not only co-ordinate marine rescue activities but have operational control of the Coast Guard's special rescue units, comprising patrolling cutters, lifeboats, launches and shore-based hovercraft.

Although all Coast Guard units are manned by Coast Guard officers and men, Volunteer Rescue Agents give valuable service in the rescue of distressed mariners. They also assist with communications and harbour checks for persons and boats reported missing.

The practice in Australia is very similar to that of HM Coastguard with the exception that the Lighthouse Authority is a branch of the Commonwealth Department and Australia has no lifeboat service, although some States maintain rescue apparatus such as breeches buoys or similar devices.

The Australian Commonwealth Department of Transport maintains a search and rescue centre manned 24 hours-a-day in Canberra. Its function is to co-ordinate all marine search and rescue operations. There is no single authority charged with the overall responsibility for search and rescue or a Coast Guard function. This is partly due to the division of responsibility between the Australian Federal Government and the Governments of the separate constituent States under their Constitution. The States are each responsible for the safety of yachts, fishing vessels and intra-state commercial vessels licensed by them. There is a very high level of co-operation and co-ordination between the various authorities.

New Zealand has no organised coastguard service as such. It has a Search and Rescue Organisation which was set up in 1947 to deal with aircraft emergencies. Shortly afterwards this was extended to include search and rescue for persons missing or in need of assistance in mountain or bush areas and missing or endangered marine craft. Protection of the fishing industry is maintained by the Department of Agriculture, which has its own vessels for this purpose.

Responsibility for close-to-shore rescues lies with the Marine Division and the Police. Rather than maintain routine patrols of the coastline which, in relation to the land area, is very great, the vessels are brought into use as a situation or crisis or danger arises.

The Marine Division assesses all the information on the distressed or missing craft and decides what action should be taken. The officers concerned with this are professional sailors. They need a high degree of professional skill to enable them to decide from the known facts about the boat, weather and ocean currents, which area should be searched.

The Police collect information about missing craft. In Auckland and Wellington they operate police launches which carry out a lot of inshore rescue work. Police con-

Amphibious helicopter from US Coast Guard service picks up Cuban refugees from two crudely hand-made craft

trol smaller operations and, after consultation with the Marine Division, call on other members of the SAR Organisation if necessary.

Volunteers give tremendous and most efficient speedy support and are used to the full on inshore operations. New Zealand's coastline is very rugged and the seas often dangerous. The oceanic area is very large and searches are correspondingly protracted, involving day-by-day work with aircraft.

South Africa has no organisation known as 'The Coastguard'. Search and rescue is basically the responsibility of the South African Railways and Harbours under the port captain nearest to the incident, but the South African Air Force and South African Navy can be called upon to assist.

The Icelandic Coast Guard is largely concerned with Fishery Protection.

Most European nations vary a great deal in their practices. The Soviet Union have a Border Guard with vessels of a naval type. These apparently have no search and rescue function.

All European countries, so far as is known, operate helicopters for search and rescue. These are usually military aircraft. Large twin-engined helicopters are used by Danish Coastguards. These can rescue a crew of fourteen from a motor vessel in distress.

A number of European countries provide special ships to support their fishing fleets. The Dutch have the *De Hoop*, which has accommodation for twelve patients in its hospital and also carries fuel and stores for transfer to fishing vessels; they also have two research vessels. These patrol in the North and Irish Seas, off the Norwegian coast and in the waters of Iceland, Greenland, Newfoundland and Labrador. They operate in much the same way as support vessels of other countries.

Britain has very close relations with Western European countries in search and rescue operations, contacting them by telex when there is anything to discuss of mutual interest. Senior officers of HM Coastguard are encouraged to visit coastguards in other countries to see the way they function and to offer opportunities for return visits to this country.

'Truly international in response, search and rescue evokes the best traditions of sea, air and radio.'*

* Quoted from *Usque ad Mare,* a History of the Canadian Coast Guard and Marine Services published by the Canadian Ministry of Transport in 1968.

3
HM Coastguard

Smuggling, as everyone knows, still exists, and in a variety of forms, but it is no longer the duty of the Coastguard to combat it. No longer do coastguard officers go in fear of their lives. Instead, they *save* thousands of lives and they depend to a great extent on the public to keep them informed of people or vessels at risk. One way in which this is done is by the use of the telephone emergency call. All telephone kiosks in British coastal areas have direct access to coastguard rescue headquarters in the same way as for police and fire calls.

Polruan Coastguard Station, built in local stone and overlooking the River Fowey

Coastguards do a lot of routine work in the shelter of their look-out operations room, or rescue headquarters, yet, at the same time, they have to be on the alert to deal with the various types of emergency which may arise at any time. Rarely does a day pass without some rescue operation being set in motion. In the summer season there may be five or six in a day at holiday resorts. During the 12 months ending March 1973 a total of 4,460 incidents of one kind and another were recorded by HM Coastguard stations around the British coast. As a result well over 4,000 people were rescued.

For coastguard purposes the 2,500 miles of Britain's coastline is divided into eleven divisions, each with its own divisional inspector, with a district officer in charge of each of the two or three districts in the division (see map on page 18). Station officers are in charge of each station with a varying number of regular and auxiliary coastguards to assist in manning them. These stations are placed at strategic points around the coast and are approximately 10 miles distant from each other where small ship traffic is heavy and runs close to the coast.

Coastguard divisions not only cover the coastline, but they stretch considerable distances out to sea. For example, the inspector of the St Ives Division in Cornwall is responsible for search and rescue as far as the north of Spain in one direction, and from Plymouth Sound due south to the French coast and along the north coast of France.

Perched high up on cliff-tops—and sometimes on concrete towers—coastguard stations have the most modern communications media. Every station is equipped with VHF radio and telephone, while rescue headquarters also have telex machines. Some stations have radar which assists in locating the position of a vessel.

Constant watch is kept day and night in greater risk

The coastguard today makes use of radio, telephone and teleprinter in his communications work

areas while stations in lower risk places have special, or day watch. Special watch is also done by auxiliary coast-guards who, in Great Britain, number 7,000. There are 600 regular coastguards. All districts have rescue headquarters constantly manned.

With few exceptions only men with several years of seagoing experience can become regular coastguards. In the past the coastguard service was staffed entirely by officers who had retired from the navy or merchant service. Now, even men of twenty-four, with shorter sea service, are encouraged to join provided they have the qualifi-

The Chief Inspector of HM Coastguard, Lt-Cdr J. A. Douglas, MBE, RN (Retd), in Calshot Coast Rescue Headquarters. In front of him (l to r) are digital clock, windspeed indicator, telephone (with switchboard) and VHF radio

cations and potential to undertake this sort of work. Younger men, without this kind of experience, who have a wish to assist in life-saving, can join as auxiliaries, though much of the auxiliary staff is comprised of those who have had some experience of the sea or communications.

The difference in rank of regular officers of HM Coastguard is shown by the amount of gold braid on their uniforms. The Chief Inspector has two broad bands and two narrow strips of braid round the sleeves, while his deputy has one broad band and three narrow strips of braid. Inspectors have four strips, district officers three, station officers two and regular coastguards only one. The

Chief Inspector and his deputy also have two rows of gold braid and oak leaves on their white peak caps, while inspectors have one and oak leaves. Other officers have the ordinary peak cap with no braid or oak leaves.

Regular coastguards have to be capable of using charts, as well as communicating machines and equipment such as radio and telex. They have to be capable of cliff climbing, be able to splice ropes, tie knots, and demonstrate a sound knowledge of other nautical skills. The 7,000 part-time auxiliary coastguards do a most useful job and are very dedicated. Without them the service could not function with the same efficiency. Some are retired people and others are engaged in all kinds of professions and trades during the day. When on patrol they have cliff-rescue equipment in the back of the 'mobile' and may be diverted to an incident and have to take charge until the regular coastguard arrives on the scene.

Stations vary greatly in the number of auxiliaries employed. In general they are in charge of rescue equipment and if a station has heavy breeches buoy gear, twenty auxiliaries will be required to set it up and use it. The work is more or less voluntary, only small sums being paid for attendance at incidents or exercises. Women also are employed as auxiliaries. At some stations they drive 'mobiles' and operate radio and telex. They log all small boats which come in and out, do filing and type reports. At Lundy Island casualty station almost half the company are women.

In the past recruits entering as regular coastguards have been sent direct to the station selected and learned the work while doing the job, but in October 1971, the first coastguard school was opened in Brixham, Devon. All newly appointed officers now go direct to their stations for a short time and then to the school for a 4-week period

Coastguards learning how to handle inflatable rescue boats at the Training School, Brixham

of training. Those officers who are seeking promotion, or needing to become acquainted with any new equipment, attend one- or two-week courses.

The school is housed in the headquarters of Southern Division, at Kings Quay, Brixham, with the rescue headquarters close at hand on Berry Head. While one group is out in the harbour with inflatable boats, being trained in launching and rescuing, another class may be in the training school doing simulated exercises in co-ordinating search and rescue services. The lone man cliff-rescue technique is demonstrated at Berry Head on another day, using equipment which can all be stowed in a small haversack. With this equipment a coastguard can safely and very quickly climb down a steep cliff in a series of hops and give first aid and reassurance to the casualty while waiting for further assistance to arrive.

The initial period of training only covers groundwork.

Recruits are instructed by their station officer and district officer during the next seven or eight months. Then they return to the school for a further fortnight. This is largely a refresher course. At the end of the fortnight their own inspector and district officer give them a proficiency test at their station. If they pass they are qualified as coastguard officers. Until they pass the test they are only temporary coastguard officers.

The United States Coast Guard has had a training centre since 1876. At that time it was housed in the revenue cutter *Dobbin*, in Massachusetts. Only a small class of cadets took a very limited training which was aimed at making them efficient ship's officers. With the increasing

One-man cliff-rescue

variety of the Coast Guard's responsibilities, the training centre was moved and the curriculum broadened until, in 1932, the Coast Guard Academy was built and opened. Today it is stated to be one of the most attractive educational establishments in the country.

Most of the regular Coast Guard officers undergo an arduous 4-year course here. Entry is through a nation-wide competitive examination. Sea duty, including search and rescue, is only one side of the training. The programme is so full that students have to be up soon after 6 o'clock in the morning and are fully occupied until 11 o'clock at night all through the four years of their training.

Coming in at eighteen, straight from high school, they can acquire a Bachelor of Science degree by the time they leave the Academy. They are then given commissions in the United States Coast Guard as officers. Because it is also a military service they are obliged to stay in the service for five years after they finish their training.

In spite of the long and rigorous training demanded, the Coast Guard has never had any trouble in getting enough recruits. This is doubtless because it is a challenging career and all coastguards are given a large amount of responsibility very early in life. This applies as much to coastguards in this country as it does to those in the United States and elsewhere.

HM Coastguard is responsible for the co-ordination of all search and rescue round the coast of Great Britain and Northern Ireland. Coastguards at rescue headquarters keep watch for vessels or people in distress and alert rescue services. A duty officer using Dopel binoculars can sight ships when they are up to 4 miles away. There are not as many vessels in trouble as there were in the old days of sailing ships, but sudden storms, collisions or shifting cargo can put a vessel at risk. When this happens the coastguard

A smoke signal giving off a volume of ORANGE coloured smoke

Slowly and repeatedly raising and lowering outstretched arms

A signal made by radio or other method consisting of the group SOS ···———··· or spoken word 'MAYDAY'

Rockets or shells throwing RED stars singly at short intervals (from aircraft a single RED pyrotechnic light fired singly or in succession)

A rocket parachute flare or a hand flare showing a RED light (from aircraft a parachute flare showing a RED light)

A continuous sounding with any fog signal apparatus

Flames on the vessel (as from a burning tar barrel, oil barrel etc.)

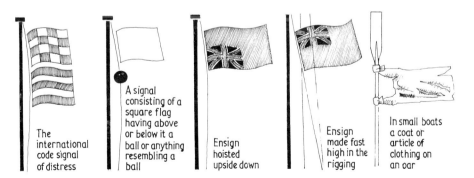

The international code signal of distress

A signal consisting of a square flag having above or below it a ball or anything resembling a ball

Ensign hoisted upside down

Ensign made fast high in the rigging

In small boats a coat or article of clothing on an oar

Distress signals

33

flashes a U warning signal to the ship, which means—
You are standing into danger. If there is no response to this
a maroon is fired.

The Master of the ship is primarily responsible for the
safety of passengers and crew. He may alert the coastguard
by a distress signal, a flare, telephone call or by a *Mayday*
call through a Post Office radio station. Messages from
ships to Post Office radio stations are often intercepted
by Coastguard listening stations who maintain a 24-hour
radio monitoring service. If information is received of a
ship in trouble it is automatically re-broadcast to other
stations. *Mayday* is a corruption of *M'aidez,* which is
French for *Help me.*

When a ship is in distress the first duty of the rescue
headquarters is to alert and record its position. While
this is being done other officers alert the necessary life-
saving services by VHF radio and telephone. The duty
officer shoulders the responsibility of deciding what is
required in such an event and takes immediate life-saving
action. He has to consider the nature of the emergency and
advise his district officer of the steps he has taken to deal
with it. If there are lives at risk he may alert the lifeboat
or helicopter. While he is doing this another officer plots
the position of the ship and decides the best rendezvous
for the lifeboat or helicopter. When plotting the position
allowance has to be made for drift, tide and wind.

Coastguards work closely with the marine insurance
agency. They know which other ships are in the vicinity
and may contact them by radio if they are likely to be
able to assist. It is obligatory for ships in the vicinity to
answer such a call for help.

If all other methods of sending help to a ship fail,
the coastguard can arrange for a radio broadcast. This may
be done at the end of the weather forecast. Some time

ago a gale in the north of Scotland blew down all telephone wires. Trees were blown across the railway. A radio *Mayday* call was received by the coastguard that three vessels in the Moray Firth were in distress and the *Princess Victoria* had sunk. Because of weather conditions the coastguard was unable to contact the lifeboat or any other rescue service in the vicinity. He, therefore, arranged for a broadcast message: 'If there is any person in the vicinity of the Cromarty lifeboat please advise them to launch.' Someone heard the broadcast, went to the lifeboat station, and action was immediately taken.

If medical assistance is required the duty officer will call a doctor who can be put in direct contact with the ship by radio telephone. This is known as a *link call*. The doctor can speak through his telephone with the captain of the ship and get exact details of where the ship is and find out what is wrong. He can give any advice which is necessary or arrange to go out to the ship by helicopter. While he is flying out the coastguard will ring the hospital and alert the ambulance. At the coastguard helicopter station at Manston in Kent, three young doctors, who give medical service voluntarily, are available at very short notice to fly in the coastguard helicopter and be lowered by winch to the deck of a ship to attend to injured or sick seamen. They are also prepared to be lowered to inaccessible parts of the coast to attend any injured person who may have fallen from cliffs. To ensure that no time is lost in getting a doctor to a patient, all have a cliff-top rendezvous near their surgeries and homes where the helicopter can pick them up. In just over a year since its inauguration, in June 1971, the unit had flown 181 rescue missions and had saved 61 lives.

Coastguards are on the alert not only for signs of distress from the larger vessels, but also from yachts and

small pleasure boats and fishing trawlers. They keep a look-out to see whether local boats are overloaded with passengers. They report to the local marine survey office if fishing vessels are not properly marked when going to sea. They watch for oil slicks, and skin-divers who have not surfaced. They watch cliffs and beaches for people in difficulties.

Every week coastguards make a special search of the beach and general coast for pollutants of one kind or another. If there is a gale, they will search again the next day to make sure nothing has come ashore. Every year, just before Easter, when what is known to coastguards as the *silly season* begins, they make a thorough search of the beaches to ensure that they are clean and clear for holiday makers. If anyone sees a vessel discharging oil they should inform the coastguard officer, who will plot the chart to find out which beaches it may pollute. He will then inform the local council. The coastguard does not deal with birds affected by oil, but he will report this to the right authority. Coastguards do, however, have responsibility for any *fish royal* which may be washed ashore or damaged. These include sturgeon, porpoises, dolphins and whales. Any found are sent to the Natural History Museum at South Kensington, in London.

If the Wild Bird Act is being contravened by the shooting of restricted birds, the coastguard informs the police.

While listening for radio, teleprinter or telephone messages, there are reports to be made and records to be written up. Every time a casualty is dealt with a report goes

OPPOSITE
One of the young doctors from the Flying Doctor Medical Service at Manston, Kent, being lowered from a helicopter

to the divisional officer who, in turn, reports to the Chief Inspector, HM Coastguard. There may be several hundred casualties a year in any one division.

The duty officer records visibility and weather conditions and reports these to the meteorological office at Bracknell. Some stations, such as St Mary's, in the Scilly Isles, report at hourly intervals. Others, such as The Lizard, in Cornwall, make reports every 3 hours and yet others report only twice a day. The meteorological office depends on coastguards for gale warning messages.

Coastguards not only sit and wait for emergency calls to come in but go out and look for people in trouble. Land-Rovers and cars are provided for this purpose. Local knowledge tells the coastguard where to go.

The coastguard film, which has been made for the use of schools and public meetings, gives a typical example of this.

The coastguard is shown on the cliff-top with a 'mobile' when a boy runs up to him.

'Help! Hi! Quick! There's a man stuck on cliff over there!'

'Right. Hop in.'

In the film the commentator points out that it might be somebody cut off by the tide; it might be a small boy after seagulls' eggs; or perhaps a would-be mountaineer overcome by fright and unable to go up or down.

When the two reach the cliff the boy points out the place where the man has fallen. The coastguard tells the boy to stand back from the cliff-edge. Then he calls on the loudhailer to the young man down below.

'Ahoy there! Coastguard here. We'll be down with you in a few minutes. Hang on. OK?'

He then uses his radio to call coastguard control.

'This is Mobile one. Do you read? Over.'

'Mobile one, this is coastguard control.'

'Control. Mobile. I am in position 665178. Man over the cliff. I'm going over alone and need cliff-team assistance.'

'Check position 665178. Will call up cliff-team at once.'

The commentator then explains that this single-man cliff-rescue method has been developed from the latest mountaineering techniques, and the essence is to be able to get to the person in trouble as quickly as possible, without having to wait for help or to rely on help from bystanders.

The coastguard has been busily hammering stakes into the ground near the edge of the cliff and securing lines to these. Now he calls to the man to reassure him.

'Right-o, son. Be with you in a minute—shan't be two seconds.' He throws one end of the line over and down the cliff. 'Hold that line. Hang on there. I'm with you now. I'll soon have you safe. Just hold on to that. There you are.'

While he is speaking he fastens the end of the lines securely round his waist and gripping the line swings himself over the cliff, letting himself down on the rope. He wears a helmet and takes a spare one and a safety-harness for the man to be rescued.

'Keep your head down,' he says. 'Tuck it well in. We'll have you out of here in no time at all now.'

He fixes the harness under the man's armpits and gives· him the helmet. But the man shows anxiety.

'This won't slip, will it?'

'That's safe as houses. Now you're all right. Just relax, son.'

The coastguard supports the man against the cliff while he listens to the radio call coming in.

'Mobile patrol. Mobile patrol. This is cliff-rescue. How do you read? Over.'

'Hallo, cliff-team. Rescue one down here. I've got a man here on a ledge about 150 feet down. He's not hurt—just exhausted. OK over.'

'Patrol. Roger. Received that, and I see your position. Will send the lines down. We should be down with you in 10 minutes. Out.'

'Roger. Try and get them down the gully. That's it. Right.'

As help comes the commentator explains that coastguard techniques are changing all the time to meet new requirements. Each cliff-rescue is different. They may have to call for ambulances and doctors, helicopters and even an inshore rescue boat to evacuate the casualty by sea. The service is flexible and, incidentally, the casualty could just as well be a sheep or a dog or a goat as a human being.

Meanwhile the coastguard, supporting the man, has been climbing the rope ladder which has been let down.

'Up you come. There you are, mate. OK?'

And another rescue has been achieved.

Covered trailers for the stowage or transport of rescue equipment are linked to these Land-Rovers when proceeding to an emergency. These trailers are also useful as shelter at the scene of the casualty.

Some stations have inflatable rubber dinghies which can be used for patrol. These have the advantage that they can quickly be launched in an emergency.

In one station alone about 230 incidents were recorded from August 1972 to March 1973. The following examples, extracted from the records, show the wide variety of incidents covered in that period. Missing person, bather in difficulties, cliff accident, skin-diver not surfaced, yacht in danger, pleasure craft missing, person signalling cut off

Land-Rovers, carrying inflatable rescue boats and towing trailers full of cliff-rescue equipment, are widely used by the coastguard today

by the tide, bodies found, animal rescue, bather in difficulty on lilo, overdue boat, canoe overturned, fishing vessel in trouble.

The fishing fleet has been much in the news and the coastguard has a special responsibility for those trawlers. In 1968 two British trawlers were lost off Iceland and as a result the coastguard have a fishery support vessel which is sent out each winter to give weather advice and medical aid to trawlers fishing in Icelandic waters.

Again, as a result of a calamity in the shipping lanes in the Dover Strait, a special sea surveillance by radar was inaugurated at St Margaret's Bay.

Further details of these and other services are given in the following chapters.

4
Search and Rescue

In the winter of 1962 the coastguard at St Just flashed a warning signal as a vessel steamed rather too close to the rocks off Cape Cornwall at the south-western tip of England. He watched as she turned, apparently heading for Sennen Cove. Then she stopped.

Unable to decide why, the coastguard contacted the Sennen rescue headquarters and asked them to investigate. While he continued his watch, the vessel fired a red flare. That confirmed his fears. She was in trouble. Immediately he took action. He radioed the Sennen life-saving company and called his district officer. As he continued his watch he received a message from the ship. She was the French trawler *Jeanne Gougy*.

By this time the district officer had arrived with two other coastguards and shortly afterwards another fifteen men joined them. Very soon they found the ship lying on her side with 20-foot breakers sweeping over her every few minutes. It was obviously impossible to do anything to help until the tide changed. Neither lifeboat nor helicopter could reach her while these conditions lasted.

The Coastguard Auxiliary Rescue Company on the cliff-top tried firing a line across to her, but when two of her crew tried to reach it they were swept overboard and drowned.

For 7 hours the vessel lay there helpless. The coastguards and life-savers watched and waited. They had no idea whether any of the crew were still on board and alive, but they had their life-saving equipment set up so that they were ready for immediate action when the time came. The hours ticked away. The coastguards had almost given up hope. No one could be alive on the stricken vessel. It would be a matter of searching for bodies.

Suddenly one coastguard called: 'There's someone in the wheelhouse. I can just see him moving his hand.'

Hope revived and at once things began to happen. The district officer contacted the crew of the RAF helicopter which was standing by in the nearest car park, and asked them to try to rescue the man.

As the wind dropped four other men came up from below and were seen clinging to the ship's rail, looking to the cliff top for help. Quickly the coastguards rigged the breeches buoy, eased both whips and dropped it on the forecastle. In less than 20 minutes the four men were all ashore. They had been trapped for nearly 7 hours, up to their chests in water, their heads in an airpocket.

At the same time the flight-sergeant winchman of the helicopter was lowered to the exhausted man in the wheelhouse. He put the strop around the casualty and the navigator did a double lift.

But the drama was not ended. The helicopter made two more attempts at rescue. On the second descent the sergeant brought out a sixteen-year-old cabin boy whom he found in a passageway behind the bridge. On the third attempt the winchman found no more survivors. The two rescued by helicopter were taken to West Cornwall hospital. All the men rescued survived the ordeal, but the master of the ship and twelve of the crew were drowned. The coastguard who first sighted the vessel was commended for a first-class piece of watch-keeping and the helicopter sergeant was awarded the George medal. The

coastguard whose watch was so effective did not even mention the rescue when the author visited his station.

It is for this kind of rescue—between shore and ship aground—that the breeches buoy is so useful. It is always used when it is dangerous for the crew to stay on board and when it is not safe for the lifeboat to go out.

All regular stations and every auxiliary station has its breeches buoy as a very important part of its rescue equipment. The rocket is fired to take a light line across to the ship. Heavier equipment follows, making a link between ship and shore. Twenty men form a rescue company and all are needed when the breeches buoy is in use. Ten men pull the hawser and all have their specific tasks. The rocket weighs 17 pounds and travels 500 yards in $2\frac{1}{2}$ seconds. It depends on the crew on board the vessel how long it takes to get the breeches buoy out. This can be in a matter of ten minutes. Vessels are provided with a tally board in French, German, Norwegian and English explaining what to do when the breeches buoy is sent out.

A wire line is attached to the gun to prevent the rope line from being burnt when the rocket is ignited. When out of use the line is neatly and expertly folded into a box so that both ends are easily obtained. The near end of the line is passed to the back of the whip and a metal float is tied to it. There are 500 yards of $1\frac{1}{2}$-inch rope.

Smaller rockets are used for vessels in distress nearer the coast, with a correspondingly smaller quantity of line.

Equipment includes a searchlight with a portable generator for working in the dark, cliff helmets with lights, similar to miners' helmets, a tripod, spikes, hammers,

OPPOSITE
Cliff-rescue from ship at sea by breeches buoy

Breeches buoy equipment

6 pound pistol and rocket

Breeches buoy

picks and shovels and a *scotsman*. This last is the name given to pieces of hide, wood or iron which are placed below the ropes to prevent them being chafed on rocks or earth.

These items are stored in all coastguard stations with other equipment ready for immediate use. When a crisis occurs they are speedily loaded into the coastguard Land-Rover or trailer. There are also parachute flares in case they are needed for searching at night. These go up to 1,200 feet and burn for two or three minutes. When there is an emergency a maroon is fired to call the rescue company.

Other equipment stored at coastguard stations, or kept in readiness in vans, includes oil skins for use of coastguards if there is a gale blowing, cliff-climbing gear, ladders and normal first-aid equipment. *Neil Robinson* stretchers made of cane and canvas are provided to bring injured seamen up through hatches in ships, up cliffs, or for hauling casualties into helicopters. Cliff-lines and ladders are often required for rescue of people from vessels driven too close to the cliffs.

One such incident occurred at Dollar Cove, on the south side of Sennen headland in the Land's End area. It happened on a bleak Sunday in November 1972, shortly after 3 o'clock in the morning. Dense fog swirling over the sea, worsened by drizzling rain, would have made watch-keeping even in daylight impossible so far as visibility was concerned. There was no chance of the officer on duty at Land's End rescue headquarters sighting any vessel requiring assistance. Yet this was one of the mornings when anything might happen. The coastguard wrote up his reports, one ear cocked for any message which might concern him.

Suddenly it came.

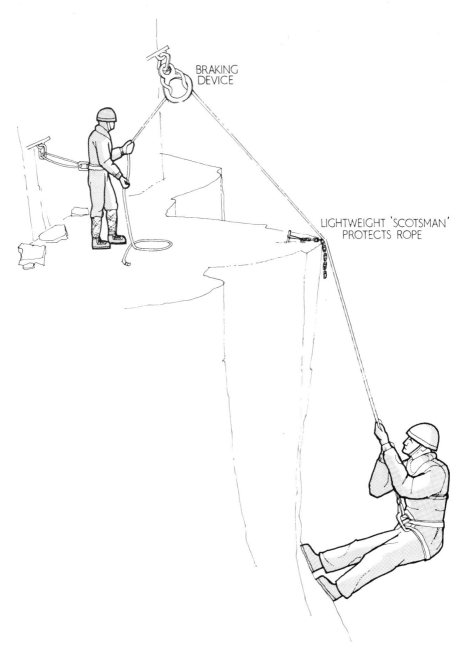

BRAKING
DEVICE

LIGHTWEIGHT 'SCOTSMAN'
PROTECTS ROPE

Coastguard being lowered, secured by chest and seat slings

'*Mayday! Mayday! Mayday!*'

The coastguard pulled pen and pad towards him as he listened.

'Land's End radio. Can I help you? Over.'

'Land's End radio. Cypriot ship *Nefali* here. We're aground on the Longships and need assistance. Must leave ship now.'

Immediately the coastguard put a call through to the Secretary of Penlee lifeboat station and advised them to launch. Then he called out the Sennen Auxiliary Coastguard Rescue Comany. They made a very fast turn out and were ordered to Land's End area to locate the ship's boats. But conditions for a search could not have been worse. The fog showed no sign of lifting and that and the drizzle added to their problems. The steep slopes of the cliff were greasy, making search hazardous. The state of the tide and the casualty position reported suggested that any boats would be drifting towards Gwennap Head. More help was required and the Tol-pedn-Penwith Coastguard Rescue Company was called. In response to a message put out to all ships in the area, two warships and a Trinity House vessel joined in the search.

It took 45 minutes to locate the stricken ship because she was totally blacked out and lay with her bows to the shore in Dollar Cove. No one knew whether she had, in fact, been abandoned. Then they heard shouts, not from the boat but from two of the vessel's crew who were trying to climb the cliff.

When the rescue team had assisted the men to the cliff top they said that the master and one of the crew were still on the ship. The rest of the crew had left the vessel over the bows by the jumping ladder and were now at the foot of the cliff in a very dangerous position, with the sea washing over them. The ship's lifeboat had been smashed as they tried to launch her. Ten of the crew were brought up the ladders to safety.

Cliff-lines and ladders were soon rigged down the steep grass bank and over the sheer drop. One of the rescue company went down to assist the survivors up the stiff slope. All were wet, cold and exhausted. Two were taken to hospital and the rest were given food and shelter by a local resident.

The whole rescue operation was difficult and dangerous but twelve lives were saved.

Another incident in the same area involved a girl and her father who had been clambering over some rocks at the base of the cliffs when the girl was swept away by the heavy sea. Her father dived after her and with considerable difficulty managed to get her on to a rock some way out to sea. Waves washed over and around them as they clung to the rock. Fortunately they were seen by a holiday-maker on the cliff-top and the coastguard rescue service was alerted.

The Sennen lifeboat was called out and rushed to the scene with a dinghy in tow. The tide was rising swiftly and huge waves were beating over the rock where the man and the girl were desperately holding on. In less than two hours the tide would reach the highest point of the year.

The St Just Coastguard cliff rescue team worked feverishly with the lifeboat crew. Together they managed to get a line across to the stranded couple. When they jumped into the water and were pulled to the base of the cliff they had endured two hours of torment on the rock. They were taken to Penzance hospital and treated for abrasions and shock before being allowed to go home.

Examples of other incidents in different coastal areas which show how the coastguard co-ordinate the rescue services are taken from the annual report

(1972/3) of the Chief Inspector, HM Coastguard.

The Hull trawler *Cassio* informed Coastguard Stornoway by link call that the German Hospital ship *Poseidon* had a critically sick man on board who needed to be lifted off and taken to hospital. The ship was then in position 160 miles west of Benbecula, Outer Hebrides. Ten minutes later aircraft assistance was requested by the Coastguard and all details of position and weather were passed. Shortly afterwards Coastguard Stornoway was informed that a long-range helicopter would take off from Aberdeen early next morning and refuel at Stornoway. All arrangements were made by the coastguard, including arrangements for a doctor with a supply of oxygen to meet the helicopter at Stornoway. The helicopter arrived at 5 o'clock the next morning, refuelled and was soon in contact on VHF with *Poseidon* on Channel 16. Lift-off was completed before 8 o'clock. They were met by an ambulance on return to Stornoway, and the patient was taken to hospital.

This is just one example from North Scotland Division of the smooth handling of a long-range medico and the excellent co-operation between Rescue Headquarters Stornoway, District Headquarters Aberdeen, the trawler *Cassio,* the German ship *Poseidon* and the helicopter crew.

Police and coastguards often co-operate as in the case of an incident at Whitby, in the North Eastern Division. On an October evening, about an hour before high tide, the Coastguard Rescue Headquarters at Aberdeen received a message from the police that two adults in charge of seven teenage students were overdue on a beach walk from Robin Hood's Bay to Whitby. It was assumed that they were under the cliffs and cut off by the tide. An immediate search was organised with police, coastguards and auxiliary coastguards from Robin Hood's Bay. The lifeboat was also launched to search the cliffs and beaches from

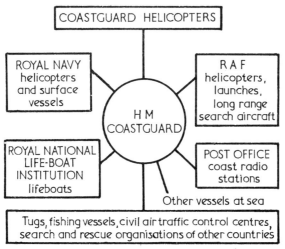

The co-ordinating role of the Coastguard

seaward as this was considered the quicker and better way of locating the stranded party. The lifeboat crew observed them beneath Whitby Lighthouse and all the searchers were directed to this position. A coastguard and an auxiliary were lowered down the 200-foot cliffs and a girl of eighteen quickly climbed the ladder which had been lowered. Other members were not so keen on climbing to such a height and during the rescue several shifts of position were made to get better climbing areas before the last person reached the cliff-top shortly before midnight, four and a half hours after the coastguard had been alerted.

On another evening Coastguard Rescue Headquarters at Aberdeen received a message from the County Police

OPPOSITE

A Royal Navy Sea King exercising with the Coverack Lifeboat

that a boy had fallen over the cliffs. A cliff-rescue team and inshore rescue boat were alerted and in ten minutes the Aberdeen mobile was on its way with the District Officer and all available staff. The inshore rescue boat was launched in spite of the fact that the sea was very rough at the mouth of the gully where the boy had fallen. Cliff gear had to be manhandled over two fences and a quarter of a mile along the railway line. Where the boy had fallen there was a steep grass slope of 140 feet, terminating in a 200-foot drop. To add to the rescuers' difficulties the boys had set fire to the dry grass. Volunteers who had gathered were given the task of beating out the fire, while the coast-guards made a guide line fast to the stakes and then to the top of the two ladders which had been joined together to give the required length. The District Officer was in constant contact with the cliff party by cliff telephone, and with the inshore rescue boat by radio. The boy appeared to be dead and the inshore rescue boat was advised not to come in as it was too risky. Two of the coastguards descended the cliff with a stretcher, having to cross a gully of water which separated them from the rock where the boy had fallen. The body was finally put on a stretcher and taken to the top of the cliff. The whole incident took three hours and called for skill and ability. It proved to be one of the most difficult cliff rescue bids recorded in this particular District.

Yet another rescue began as a result of a telephone call to Coast Rescue Headquarters, Holyhead. The caller said that cries for help were coming from a boat off Caley Promenade, Rhos-on-Sea. Llandudno Coast Rescue Company was called out and the Llandudno lifeboat launched. On arrival at the scene the auxiliary coastguard in charge at Llandudno saw an open fishing boat going round in circles, and heard the occupants shouting for help. Unsuccessful attempts were made to instruct the occupants by loudhailer to head out to sea, shut down the engine and await the lifeboat, as they were in danger of striking a submerged wooden groyne or a rock. Shortly afterwards the boat struck a groyne and the occupants were thrown out of the boat which sank immediately. Two auxiliary coastguards and two police officers swam out to the two occupants and brought them safely ashore. It was a hazardous undertaking due to the rocky nature of the coast and the large amount of debris that was thrown up in the heavy surf, with a north-easterly wind and rough sea. The occupants, both fourteen years old, had stolen the boat from Rhyl. The four rescuers were awarded the Royal Humane Society's Testimonial on Vellum.

A more unusual rescue took place after a message was received by Coastguard Castletown, in the Northern Ireland Division, that a Naval Survey party had seen a boy go into a disused mine-shaft at the bottom of the cliffs at Bradda Head, and it was thought likely that he had been trapped. The Castletown staff and the Port Erin Coastguard Rescue Company left for Bradda Head. The mine-shaft could only be reached from the top of the 350-foot cliffs by a crumbling and dangerous path. The rescue party made their way down carrying their cliff equipment. At the bottom they found the boy outside the mine-shaft unharmed. He told them that his dog had run into the mine and fallen down a vertical shaft.

Darkness was approaching and the boy was evacuated by a small boat. It was then discovered that the boy's aunt, who had been at the top of the cliff, was missing and a search of the cliff face was started. She was soon found and helped to the top.

The tide was too far in for any attempt to be made to rescue the dog, but on the following morning the team went by boat to the entrance to the mine. They worked their way in along the horizontal shaft for about 50 feet until they came to the vertical shaft down which the dog had fallen. They proceeded to drive stakes into the floor of the gallery, buttoned up a cliff-ladder and cliff-line to the stakes and an auxiliary coastguard was lowered to the bottom, a matter of some 40 feet. There, in 3 feet of water, with a dead sheep and other rubbish, was Breck, a Border collie, alive and apparently unharmed. After a struggle in the darkness and filth, the coastguard managed to put the dog into a sling made of an old fishing net. The dog was hauled to safety and the team returned to Port Erin by boat, where Breck was reunited with his overjoyed family. After a shampoo he appeared none the worse for his ordeal.

Beach guards employed by local councils are concerned for the safety of swimmers. They work very closely with the coastguard and if they cannot handle any situation they telephone for assistance.

A very gallant rescue was undertaken by a sixteen-year-old Southend-on-Sea boy, who had joined the auxiliary coastguard when the age limit was reduced. He was on watch on the pier one night when he heard cries for help. He ran to the eastern side of the pier and looked down. It was too dark to see anyone in the water. Flares were fired and immediately the boy dived 20 feet into the water.

He found a girl was being swept out to sea by the tide. With some difficulty he managed to support her and calm her fears. The tide carried them both further from the pier and it began to look as though both would drown. Then the boy remembered his scout training. He removed his trousers and tied a knot in each of the legs. He managed to blow into the top of the trousers until they were filled with air, like water-wings. Tying a knot in the top of the trousers he tucked them under his armpits.

Both were rescued by the senior coastguard on duty in a rowing boat who used his local knowledge to go to the right spot. The auxiliary coastguard concerned was awarded the British Empire Medal for gallantry and received it from the Queen at Buckingham Palace.

Another incident of an entirely different kind resulted from the sinking of the Spanish motor vessel *Germania*. She sank after a fire and explosion 75 miles from Fowey, in Cornwall. This became known to coastguards as *operation drumbeat*. It began with a member of the public informing the Mevagissy coastguard that two or more 45-gallon drums were ashore at St Austell.

Now these drums could be dangerous or inflammable. They might contain oil or other pollutant for all the coastguard knew. It was their job to see that they were salvaged and examined. First they had to inform emergency services and other interested authorities. Then the shipping authorities had to be contacted. Telex, radio and telephone were in constant use. All coastguards, regular and auxiliary, patrolled the coast from Rame Head to Padstow, each team being given a particular area for search. In the team with the coastguards were scientists and bomb and mine disposal units.

The whole area was searched on foot, by boat or by helicopter. Operations were controlled from the Falmouth Rescue Headquarters, by the Inspector of the Division and the District Officer, who also conferred with the Truro oil pollution control centre set up by Cornwall County Council.

Reports of more and more drums being located came in over the next few days as regular and auxiliary coastguards in the district made long and hazardous coast searches. The operation lasted from 13 to 25 January. During that

time rescue headquarters at Falmouth was constantly manned by additional regular and auxiliary staff. They provided telex, telephone and radio communications, acted as a link between the teams in the field and the emergency control centre at Truro. They plotted all drum positions and kept in contact with the Culdrose Naval Air Station who were locating and lifting the drums by helicopter.

Some drums were found empty and others were leaking. By the end of the operation about 200 drums had been found. Sixty-six were exploded and special drum dumps were set up for the disposal of others.

OPPOSITE

Operation Drumbeat 1972. Recovering a drum of chemicals washed ashore on a Cornish beach. The drums were airlifted to a dump, and then destroyed

5
Helicopters and Trawlers

Helicopters

We have already seen how useful helicopters can be in search and rescue operations. Some military air stations situated near the sea have their own search and rescue helicopters with crews on call for military emergencies. Military authorities work closely with the coastguard, lifting from the beaches stranded holiday visitors cut off by the tide and picking up crews from capsized dinghies. Helicopters are particularly useful for cliff rescues because they can come down close to the casualty. This is a skilful and hazardous task. One false move could cost the lives of the whole crew.

One instance of such a rescue occurred in Britain in September 1971. The klaxon alert sounded as a call came over the loudspeaker at Culdrose: 'Scramble the SAR.'

This was a call for action. Within two minutes the crew on duty were airborne and on their way, getting their instructions over the radio as they went. They were told that a woman had fallen from the cliffs and was lying seriously injured in a *bowl* in the undercliff. Slowly and carefully the pilot manoeuvred his plane far enough into the undercliff for the leading air mechanic to be lowered with a stretcher. Then the helicopter flew away while two ambulance men and two skin-divers took the stretcher to the woman and splinted and bandaged her. When the helicopter returned she was strapped on the stretcher ready to be lifted and flown to West Cornwall hospital in Penz-

With rescue bracket lowered, a helicopter hovers over a grounded motorboat and two men in rough surf

ance, where nurses were waiting on the cricket ground adjacent to the hospital as the helicopter landed.

This is only one instance of many rescues carried out by military helicopters from many different airports.

Where there is no military air station, the Coastguard has its own helicopter search and rescue base. At Manston in Kent, such a service is supplied by Bristows, the world's leading operators of helicopters, but it comes under the Coastguard authorities. The drill is much the same for military helicopters.

The crew consists of the pilot, a winchman and a navigator. All wear helmets with earphones and microphones built in. They have life-jackets which go over the head and tie round the body.

Every pilot is qualified to winch. They have to do a certain number of hours of actual flying each month, which includes the amount done on incidents. They practise cliff-operation and hovering over the sea. While exercising they fly out, mark and drop an object and go in and find it. Accuracy is very important. If the pilot is one degree out in 60 miles he will be in the wrong position by one mile, which could make a considerable difference in finding the target.

Double lift from sea by Manston helicopter crew

The navigator is trained to guide the plane and operate the winch, but he is not a diver. He sits in the aircraft below and behind the pilot and works out the direction and speed of the wind and how it is affecting the helicopter. He writes this down and hands the paper to the pilot, who makes the final decision. It is the navigator's job to despatch the winchman (who may be a trained diver) but he must ask the pilot's permission before doing so. If the helicopter is flying too fast, or too high, the pilot may decide it is not the right time to go down. He is in charge of the plane and his decision is final.

The winchman is fully trained in search and rescue and can jump from the helicopter from a height of 40 feet at a speed of 5 knots or less. He can hit the water within about 20 seconds of leaving the helicopter. He carries a whistle and wears a safety belt to give him freedom of movement. When he is ready to be winched up with a casualty he sits in a small canvas seat attached to the winching strop and supports the casualty (who is also hooked to the strop), with his legs.

People cannot be winched in complete darkness but if there is a moon, lights on shore, or the horizon is visible, searches can be made. The United States Coast Guard, however, have a high-intensity 'night sun' light fitted to some of their helicopters. With this in use survivors have been spotted and rescued on really dark nights.

Crews keep in touch with their base and can talk direct to the coastguard and the lifeboat. With still air the helicopter can travel at $1\frac{1}{2}$ miles a minute or 95 miles per hour. In the wind it takes double the time. They only carry enough fuel for a 45 minute journey to and from the station, with another 20 minutes over the sea or cliff. They do not fill up with fuel because of the additional weight they are going to pick up. They might lift three people weighing 200 pounds each, all of whom are very wet. In the event of the search being likely to take longer than the fuel will last the pilot can radio for a fixed-wing aircraft and this could be on its way in time to take over, but it cannot come down as close to the casualty as can the helicopter, nor hover in the same way.

Military and coastguard search and rescue helicopters carry much the same equipment. They are supplied with a range of maps and charts to cover at least 100 miles around the sea. Pictures of hospitals in the vicinity are provided, with details of telephone numbers and their exact position and nearest landing places. Crews are all trained in first-aid or have St John's or Red Cross certificates. Four oxygen chargers are supplied so that oxygen can be given to four people at one time. A doctor's bag has been made up by doctors for their use when flying to a medical case. This contains drugs and equipment which is more specialised than the normal first-aid kit so that casualties can be treated on the helicopter. Plastic splints and a *paraguard* rescue stretcher with head guard are provided for the diver to take down to the casualty when necessary.

Another item carried on the helicopter is a blackboard. The aircraft can go very close to a small ship and write in chalk on the board: 'Are you OK?' or 'Did you fire a flare?' or 'Do you require assistance or fuel?' or any other important message.

Trawlers

We buy our fish and chips and eat our fish dinners, seldom thinking of the fishermen who spend weeks at a time on the sea, often in very bad weather conditions. Trawlers get stranded, collide, catch fire and founder.

Those fishing in Icelandic waters are in special danger from north-east gales and below-zero temperatures, which cause icing conditions. Vital equipment may be iced up and a vessel put in danger by the sheer weight of a blanket of ice forming on it. Freezing spray causes icing alarmingly quickly. A trawler may come up against a big area of floating ice and some large pieces of *glacier ice*. These are sometimes a beautiful deep green colour and not easily distinguishable at a distance even with the use of radar. They are known to trawlermen as *growlers* and can cause a lot of damage to ships.

One of the most recent disasters occurred in February 1968 when three vessels and their crews were lost off Iceland after they had iced up and overturned in exceptionally bad weather. A coastguard officer, the present Chief Inspector of HM Coastguard, was immediately sent to Iceland in a weather ship. Trawlers fishing in such areas are in great danger, not only from weather conditions, but from their isolated position.

For many years trawlers of 80 feet and over in length, and some of the smaller vessels, had been reporting their positions to their owners each day through coast radio stations. When any failed to report, the district coastguard officer was advised and he instituted a search in case they were in trouble.

At the end of 1968, however, the British Government chartered a trawler, the *Orsino*, to stand by the Icelandic fishing fleet as a support ship. The support ship *Orsino* was to be on station off Iceland for an experimental period of 6 months. She had special radio communication facilities and a sick bay. Coastguard officers took turns in serving in the support ship, their object being to advise trawler skippers on weather and safety. A meteorologist and a doctor were also appointed.

The service came under the control of the Chief Inspector, HM Coastguard. Twice a day the *Orsino* was in radio contact with all trawlers in the area to find out whether any were in difficulties. At the same time she provided information and advice about weather conditions. The fishing trawlers themselves also supplied information about the weather in their immediate area and especially about pack-ice, icebergs and icing on board. When temperatures were below freezing, and gales were blowing, trawlers were warned to keep south of such areas, or to seek shelter. The coastguard officer also kept in touch with individual skippers who were in isolated or exceptionally dangerous positions.

Accidents often happen to fishermen when their vessels are not in danger. The men run risks of being swept away by heavy seas in gales and storms. They work in all kinds of weather on an open deck, shooting and towing their nets over the side of the boat only a few feet above the sea. They also suffer bodily accidents and bad health from the nature of their work and the medical service provided

Trawler support vessel Miranda, *which is stationed off Iceland every winter to provide British trawlers with medical and weather-advisory service*

by the Coastguard ship *Orsino* was greatly appreciated. The doctor on board was able to advise by radio-telephone whether a sick or injured man should be landed in port for treatment or whether he could be treated by the skipper. Where necessary men were transferred to the support ship for immediate treatment.

After the *Orsino* had operated for two winters in support of the fishing fleet the Department of Trade and Industry decided to purchase its own vessel to maintain a *presence* off north-west Iceland during the winter months. A Swedish-built vessel was chosen with an overall length of 237 feet, a breadth of $37\frac{1}{2}$ feet, a draught of 14 feet and a speed of 11 to 12 knots. She was named *Miranda* (after the character in Shakespeare's play *The Tempest*) who, as the daughter of Prospero, had compassion for shipwrecked sailors.

This ship is still in commission each winter. A coastguard inspector is the captain. The crew of thirty-four includes the fishery officer, meteorologist, doctor and sick-berth attendant, chief radio officer and three other radio officers.

The hospital on the trawler has a surgery and operating table, a dental chair, X-ray apparatus and a ward for six patients. It also has a dispensary and a dark room. There is a workshop with a lathe and drilling machine as well as welding facilities.

As with the *Orsino*, the *Miranda* has about an hour's 'round-up' (radio contact) with all British trawlers reporting their positions twice a day. There may be more than eighty vessels in the area at one time. The 'round-up' is followed by the weather forecast and any advice the coastguard wishes to pass on. Ships in the area are then given the opportunity to ask for any medical advice or technical service.

The positions of the trawlers are plotted and the coastguard officer in command can see the complete disposition of the British fishing fleet off Iceland. Having studied the short and longer term forecasts he may consider that the risk of icing is likely to be dangerous to certain ships. He will, in that case, advise such trawlers to seek shelter, though he cannot order skippers to take his advice. The final decision rests with them. If vessels fail to report to *Miranda*, or make it known that they are in difficulties, the coastguard arranges for search and rescue measures to be taken.

The Z boat, as the inshore rescue craft is known, is lifted over the side of the main vessel by a small electric crane. Only three men are in the boat when she is launched. If more are needed they use the jumping ladder. The Z boat can keep in touch with the support ship by means of walkie-talkie sets.

In an emergency the crew can get away in 5 minutes. They wear an orange-coloured one-piece survival suit over their ordinary suit. This is sealed at the wrists. The head and neck are protected by the draw string on the hood and neck of the suit. Extra survival suits are carried for the use of any patients who have to be transferred to *Miranda* for treatment. Normally the boat is not sent when winds are at Force 8 or more.

Although *Miranda*'s main task is to make sure the trawler and crew are safe, the technical staff carry out repairs to radio and radar sets, echo sounders, propulsion or steering gear. They can also supply spare parts when needed. The safety of the ship may depend on this. In the second season 92 such repairs were undertaken. These involved 132 boat trips.

Junior officers of the coastguard service are sometimes taken on the *Miranda* for a 3-week spell of training. One such officer gives the following account of an incident which occurred while he was on the vessel: 'We were rudely awakened at 0445 with the news that the trawler *Cassio* was on fire 15 miles north of North Cape. *Miranda* was underway in 15 minutes and arrived at the scene of the casualty at 0800. Fire was reported to be in the starboard accommodation and the area had been battened down. *Cassio* proceeded to Isafjord escorted by *Miranda* and the Icelandic coastguard vessel *Odinn*. Although the starboard accommodation was completely gutted, there were no casualties and the vessel returned to the United Kingdom.'

6
Yachts and Small Craft

'Two boys, aged five and sixteen, were rescued by coast-guard helicopter and landed on the cliff top near Margate after a dinghy from which they were fishing was caught by a gale force wind and began to drift out to sea $1\frac{1}{2}$ miles off North Foreland. A man and a little girl who were with them in the 12-foot dinghy were brought ashore by Margate lifeboat. The coastguard helicopter from Manston flew out when the dinghy was seen to be dragging anchor and drifting seawards. A crewman was put on board and found that all four occupants were suffering from seasickness. The sixteen-year-old boy was winched into the helicopter and landed on the cliff top near the coastguard look-out. Then the helicopter took the five-year-old boy to safety. The helicopter returned to the scene and stood by until the lifeboat arrived and rescued the other two.'

This newspaper account of a rescue from a dinghy caught in a gale force wind is typical of many such which are co-ordinated by the Coastguard. All through the sailing season it is the same story. People go to sea in boats without taking normal precautions. In some districts two or three boats capsize every day and there is an increasing number of sailing and motor craft on which rescue action has to be taken. In the year 1971/2 the number was over a thousand.

Sometimes accidents occur because a boat is not seaworthy. If a car breaks down on the road it is possible to walk to the nearest telephone or garage and get help. A breakdown at sea is an entirely different matter.

A thirteen-year-old Ramsgate schoolboy was rescued by helicopter one Sunday after spending a night in an open boat. He was reported missing after he failed to return from a fishing trip. The boy went fishing with the owner of a 28-foot motor cruiser which had been a ship's lifeboat. They left the harbour at 2 o'clock one Saturday afternoon and expected to return in about 2 hours. When they did not arrive the Coastguard was alerted. The officer on duty contacted the Manston helicopter station and a search was made. The boat was discovered broken down 2 miles off Deal. Fortunately they were winched to safety none the

HM Helicopter Coastguard Station at Manston Aerodrome, Kent

worse for the adventure, but they might not have been so lucky.

There have been many tragic incidents which have not ended so happily, though they have involved police as well as coastguards in a lot of work and expense.

A man reported to the coastguard at one of the Cornish stations that a car had been seen on the beach the previous day with a small boat. Now the boat had gone but the car was still there. This could be nothing serious, or it could mean that the boat had been out all night and was lost. The Coastguard takes no chances in such a case and a search was instituted.

They took the registration number of the car and asked the police if they could find out who owned it. They obtained a description of the boat from the local boat club and found that the owners lived in Sussex and had been camping, but the camp was now empty, though four people had been known to be there. Messages were put out to all coastguard stations in the area and soon an upturned boat of the same description was found well out to sea and the four people were found drowned.

If they had left a card with the local coastguard, or asked someone to telephone the coastguard if the boat had not returned by a certain time, this search could probably have been made the same day and all four lives saved. When people are on holiday and put out to sea in a boat with no-one knowing them or where they are going, this sort of thing can happen.

The Coastguard will always respond to a distress call from yachts or other small craft. If a watch can be kept, the Coastguard will do so. They were not set up for this purpose but they have assumed a large measure of responsibility for yachts and their surveillance, because it is within their capability to do so.

HM Coastguard stations situated in coastal areas where there are a lot of yachts and pleasure craft have a list of experienced yachtsmen who are willing to be called to assist in the event of an incident. They act as auxiliaries and are equipped with radio with the frequency used for search and rescue. When they are at sea they are available and equipped to help in an emergency, and they do a very useful job.

The US Coast Guard have a similar service, but their auxiliary yachtsmen assist much more extensively. This is because American Coast Guardsmen are authorised to cover a much wider range of duties. Auxiliaries who are experienced yachtsmen and own their boats assist the Coast Guard in areas where facilities may be overtaxed. At weekends in particular they will help with rescues in areas where the Coast Guard is unable to provide facilities at the time. This is done voluntarily. They are only paid for fuel which is used.

The auxiliary coastguard receiving the radio message to take his yacht to the scene of the incident

The Canadian Coast Guard has its volunteer 'search-masters'. These are people who have volunteered to take part in search and rescue duties as opportunity arises, or the Coast Guard rescue officer requests. They are owners of motor craft fitted with radio telephone and are only used when they are in control of their boat and able to proceed to a rescue at short notice. They are unpaid and receive no expenses but are allowed to hoist the official pendant—blue and white with the red maple leaf and the letters SR—when they are available.

US Coast Guard Auxiliaries run courses on such things as how to navigate, how to take care of a boat, 'rules of the sea' and the buoy system. This makes the boat-owner better equipped to go to sea and makes him a lot safer.

As a courtesy US Coast Guardsmen will also go to various marinas or wherever there is a large number of boats and ask boat-owners if they would like their craft inspected for safety. They will even go out to sea to do this. Life-saving equipment, fire-extinguishers, ventilation in the engine department and anything which will make the boat safer will be inspected. The owner will be notified of any deficiencies and when corrected, or if there are no deficiencies, the coast guardsman will give him a sticker to put in a prominent place on the vessel so that there is no need for further inspection.

There are about 7 million private boat-owners in the United States and these are growing at the rate of about half a million a year. They engage in sailing-boat and power-boat races. The auxiliaries patrol these regattas to make sure courses are not violated by the public. The Coast Guard is not there so much to protect the lives of those taking part as to protect the public against them. Power boats can do up to 70 miles per hour and could kill anyone who is in the way.

In Canada, many private citizens living on the coast act as Volunteer Rescue Agents. Many have their own boats and over the years have not only engaged in the actual rescue of distressed mariners, but have carried out harbour checks for people and boats reported missing.

Recently the New Zealand Search and Rescue Organisation set up a voluntary system involving pleasure-boatmen and fishermen. They provide search advisers with plenty of local knowledge and operational personnel who act voluntarily under the control of the Police, Marine Division and the SAR Organisation. In many areas volunteer coast guard groups have also been formed by the public to give assistance to the SAR Organisation. They drop 4-man inflatable life-rafts from privately-owned light aircraft to people in difficulties at sea. As a quick response in an emergency this has proved a valuable aid.

Lives are lost through inexperience, failure to get a

Two small-boat sailors about to make a passage round the coast of Britain hand in their completed Yacht Passage Report form to a coastguard officer

weather report and failure to seek or heed the advice given by the coastguard or other authorities who may be in a better position to judge the wisdom of proceeding on a trip or not. Unexpected dangers can be encountered at sea which cause anxiety even to the most experienced yachtsman. There may be a sudden squall or unexpected worsening in the weather. One of the crew or passengers may suddenly become ill.

Leaflets are issued by HM Coastguard giving advice on how to avoid being stranded or drowned at sea, and what to do in case of a sudden emergency.

One of the most important points at the beginning of a sailing season is to ensure that the local coastguard has full details of the boat and the safety equipment carried. This is for quick reference in case of emergency. If going on a longer voyage, full details should be given to the coastguard and also to a friend or relative ashore who will be in a position to inform the coastguard if for any reason the boat is overdue. In this way the coastguard will have a full description of the overdue boat and can quickly initiate a search and rescue operation along the route likely to have been taken by the craft.

Many lives would be saved and the coastguard's task made easier and more effective if this procedure was followed by all yachts and small craft.

HM Coastguard issues a list of precautions and safety points for boat-owners. These are:

1 Never sail without a life-jacket of approved design for every person and always have it immediately available. Wear it and/or a safety harness when there is a risk of falling overboard.
2 Tell friends ashore of your intentions: they should inform the coastguard if you are overdue.

3 Carry the safety equipment recommended for your craft, including flares, inflatable dinghy or life-raft, lifebuoys, fire-extinguishers, buckets with lanyard, anchor and chain, water-resistant torch and compass.
4 Obtain a local weather forecast and tidal information before sailing and carry a radio receiver for further forecasts.
5 Do not overload your boat when sea-angling.
6 Make sure your engine is in good order with sufficient fuel to get you back. Carry a tool kit.

The coastguard needs to be on call for those emergencies caused through no fault of the individual afloat. If small-boat-owners fail to take precautions which have been recommended, they could be occupying the coastguard's attention and time when people at greater risk are in need of them.

Signalling with an Aldis lamp to a yacht. At the left is a board showing the availability of local lifeboats

7
Danger in the Sea Lanes

Between three and four hundred ships pass through the sea lanes in Dover Strait every day. They carry about $1\frac{1}{2}$ million tons of crude oil and 15,000 tons of dangerous cargo. In fact, Dover Strait is probably the most densely populated strait in the world. In addition to ships, there may be as many as 200 cross-Channel ferries a day in the busy season.

Because of the number of collisions between ships in busy areas, the International Maritime Consultative Organisation (IMCO), the United Nations specialised agency, which acts in a maritime consultative capacity, and has its headquarters in Great Britain, produced a traffic separation scheme whereby ships throughout the world were asked to observe the 'rules of the sea' and keep to their separate lanes. Over 300 separation zones are in operation throughout the world, but traffic cannot be forced to keep to them. They can only be advised in their own and other vessels' interest to do so. One of the reasons why they do not always heed the advice is because it may save time to cross over into the other lane. Tides are all important to shipping and if a ship misses a tide she might have to wait for 8 hours for it to change again.

A very serious collision occurred in October 1970 between the *Pacific Glory* and the *Allegro*. The *Pacific Glory* was a tanker so there was serious danger of oil pollution. The Coastguard alerted all authorities and initi-

US Coast Guard cutter investigates and assists at Shell Oil Company's burning platform in Gulf of Mexico. The fire began on 1 December 1970 and was not extinguished until 12 April 1971

ated action at once.

The coastguards at Ventnor and the Needles on the Isle of Wight noticed a red glow in the sky. The next thing they saw was a ship on fire. The whole ship was ablaze from end to end. It was the tanker— the *Pacific Glory.*

Coastguards immediately went into action. Yarmouth and Bembridge lifeboats were called out, the Royal Navy, the RAF at Thorney Island, civilian fire-fighting tugs, service and private hovercraft: all were rushed to the scene of the fire. Other ships were alerted and were soon in the area. They picked up survivors from rafts and in the sea until thirty out of a crew of forty-three were saved. The importance of the Coastguard's prompt action in sighting the fire was clearly demonstrated.

It took 48 hours to get the fire under control, with fire-fighters running enormous risks as they boarded the blazing tanker.

An even more serious accident occurred in 1971 with a multiple collision between four ships. They were the *Texaco, Caribbean, Brandenberg* and *Nikki*. The first two ships collided, then another ran on top and the fourth came on top of that, with the result that many lives were lost. Not much oil was spilled although there was great

Sinking British ship Ambassador. *Wild seas make rescue operations difficult. Swimmers in rubber suits stand ready in the rescue vessel to go over the side to help survivors*

risk of this.

After that catastrophe the British Government took action. Tests were carried out to obtain some idea of traffic operation. This had never been done before. A marine traffic engineering study group was organised on which the Chief Inspector of HM Coastguard was represented. The group reached the conclusion that the traffic-separation scheme was helpful in reducing the number of collisions. St Margaret's Bay coastguard station had been closed down and moved to Deal. It was opened up again, and a radar set was installed; volunteers from the Coastguard service were called to man it. The service at St Margaret's Bay was expanded to fifteen men so that continuous 24-hour-a-day-watch could be kept on the sea lanes in the English Channel.

In September 1972 the British Government made regulations by which it was an offence for British ships to go against the prescribed direction of traffic flow in the lanes of the separation scheme.

A Channel Navigation Advisory Service was set up by HM Coastguard. This is really a radio information service warning ships of the movement of other vessels not keeping to the sea lanes. About 2,000 messages a month are broadcast. Information on new risks, such as buoys out of position or damaged or unlit, drilling, pollution or other relevant details are also passed on to ships using the sea lanes. If a tug with a tow is coming through this is reported. Since this advisory service has come into operation there have been very few serious collisions.

There have been some near misses. One such involved a fully laden 200,000-ton tanker and a cross-Channel ferry. The tanker nearly sliced the ferry in two. The coastguard at St Margaret's Bay tracked the inward-bound tanker from the time she was seen to enter the south-west lane, where she went against the traffic flow, but there was nothing anyone could do about this at the time, though a radar picture was being photographed at minute intervals. The identification of this or any other ship going the wrong way in the Channel is reported to the Government of the ship's country.

An unidentified ship hit a wreck buoy at the Varne, and a Belgian fishing boat, also off the Varne, lost her rudder through a glancing blow with an outward-bound ship.

In spite of all that is being done to keep the English Channel safe for shipping, about thirty-five ships a day contravene the regulations. A large number of these 'rogues' are fishing vessels. Cargo ships and larger vessels are mostly law abiding. Ships must keep to the lanes laid down but they can cross at an angle of ninety degrees.

The coastguard on duty plots all these ships which contravene the regulations but it is not easy to obtain sufficient evidence to bring them to court. If two ships approach each other at 15 knots in 6 minutes they have closed to one another within five miles. This does not give a great deal of time to plot and make a reliable report. Other means of policing are being experimented with, including the use of helicopters.

When all countries make similar regulations requiring their vessels to keep to the sea lanes, shipping in the Dover Strait will be much safer than it is today.

8
Warning and Rescue Services

Lighthouses, Lightships and Buoys

Although lighthouses and lightships and buoys have been established as warning signals and not for rescue purposes, no story of the sea would be complete without at least a passing reference to them. They do not come under the control of the Coastguard but liaise with them as necessary.

The Corporation of Trinity House, London, which evolved out of a Medieval Guild of Mariners, is solely responsible for the erection and maintenance of these signals of potential danger to navigation around the coast. As well as providing pilots who guide ships safely to and from British ports the Corporation maintains about 90 major lighthouses, almost 30 light-vessels and nearly 700 buoys, half of which are lighted. In addition there are numerous local seamarks in the approaches to ports and harbours. The Corporation is responsible for dealing with wrecks except those of HM ships or those which occur in local ports.

A fleet of diesel-electric lighthouse tenders are used for servicing lighthouses, buoys, towing light vessels and locating and marking wrecks. A helicopter is also used for changing men at some isolated lighthouses.

The Wolf Rock lighthouse is manned by a principal keeper and three assistants. Three of these men are always on duty. A beacon was first erected on this rock in 1791 but the sea carried it away immediately. Another beacon

Wolf Rock Lighthouse

took five years to build because owing to weather conditions there were only 302 hours in which work could be done. This was completed successfully in 1840.

Great Britain has one of the most modern lighthouses in the world. Situated on the coast at Dungeness, it came into operation in November 1961. The tower, rising 140 feet from a white concrete base, is capable of being operated automatically, though it is manned by a principal

OPPOSITE
An injured lighthouse-keeper being lifted from Wolf Rock by diver from helicopter

keeper and three assistants who live with their families close by. Apart from many other special qualities all its main navigational aids are duplicated. This means that they are automatically changed to the stand-by equipment in the event of failure.

The whole tower is floodlit, which makes it more readily seen by ships at sea. An interesting outcome of this is the reduction in the mortality rate of birds at this lighthouse in the migrating season.

The Royal Sovereign lighthouse, off Eastbourne, was commissioned in 1971. Built in two sections on the beach at Newhaven, it replaced a light-vessel. It has navigational aids which include fog signal and radio beacon as well as the light.

Great Britain has the largest fleet of light-vessels in the world, with nearly thirty still in use. These are mainly situated on the east coast and in the North Sea. Two light-vessels, together with fourteen buoys, served as wreck-warning lights to mark ther wrecks of the *Texaco, Caribbean, Brandenberg* and *Nikki,* described on page 80, in chapter 7. A new light-vessel station was also established in 1972 as part of the marking route in the Dover Strait.

Although not their specific function, Trinity House personnel contribute to search and rescue operations. Recently one of the lighthouse keepers was informed that a boy and a man were stranded 150 feet down the cliffs and cut off by the tide. The keeper alerted the coastguard

OPPOSITE

Trinity House Vessel Winston Churchill *servicing the Royal Sovereign lighthouse. (A helicopter is used for changing the crew of three keepers who spend two months on duty followed by one month ashore)*

who called out the rescue services. The cliffs were very steep and all attempts at rescue were unsuccessful until the lighthouse keeper offered to go down. When he was lowered he found the boy unconscious and the man suffering from shock. It was too dangerous to take the boy up the cliff, so his rescuer carried him through the rough sea to safety.

This is only one of the many cases where men from tenders, pilot vessels, lighthouses and light-vessels have assisted in search and rescue.

Lifeboats

Among the rescue services which co-operate with HM Coastguard and whose crews risk their lives in saving the lives of others, is the lifeboat institution. Unlike HM Coastguard this is not controlled by Government.

In 1823, soon after the Coastguard came into being under that name, Sir William Hillary wrote a pamphlet entitled *An Appeal to the British Nation on the Humanity and Policy of Forming a National Institution for the Preservation of Lives and Property from Shipwreck*. This article aroused public interest, and a year later the Royal National Life-boat Institution was formed. It was not known under that name until thirty years later. Before that its popular name was *The Shipwreck Institution*. It was started as a voluntary organisation and has remained so apart from a period of fifteen years when it was given a Government grant.

Its main aim has always been the saving of life, and in the 150 years of its existence, its volunteer crews have been responsible for saving 80,000 people from death at sea.

Lifeboats were actually invented about fifty years before the RNLI was founded, though they were very different from those in use today. In the early years boat designers experimented with many different types. Such vessels had to be strong enough to face perpetual danger from rocks and sandbanks. Lifeboat crews go to sea when most other seamen prefer to stay ashore. The main aim of boat builders was to invent a craft of such stability that it could brave the roughest and most treacherous seas and stay afloat. The ideal was that it should be unsinkable and not capsize.

By progressive steps over the years this has been achieved to a very great extent. Lifeboats today are unsinkable.

The first lifeboats were, of course, rowing boats. Even when steam began to be used it was a long time before it was found at all suitable for this purpose. Progress in the method of driving the boat continued. Today, lifeboats are driven by powerful diesel engines.

During World War II boat-building yards were engaged in other work and lifeboat development virtually ceased. There were hazards other than tempestuous seas to be faced. The Cromer lifeboat rescued no less than eighty-eight men from a convoy of six ships, while another thirty-one were rescued by other lifeboats. Whatever the nationality of the crew, whether friend or foe, lifeboats made the same effort at rescue. During the battle of Britain, German, as well as English, pilots were picked up from the sea.

Lifeboats are called out three times as often as they were even twelve years ago. This is largely due to the popularity of yachts and other sailing craft and the inexperience of owners of many of these, but also to modern methods of communication. Instead of depending on visual signals which may or may not be seen, a ship in distress only has to use its radio telephone and all rescue services will be available to assist immediately.

Modern lifeboats are equipped with radio transmitters and receivers, searchlights, loudhailers, signalling lamps, oil spray, radio direction-finding equipment, echo-sounders, and radar. They also have line-throwing pistols, stretchers, first-aid equipment and even emergency rations and pressure cookers.

The six steel lifeboats of the 44-foot class which have been built for the RNLI are stationed at Barry Dock, Dover, Dun Laoghaire, Great Yarmouth and Gorleston, Harwich and Troon. They are based on a United States design. They have great manoeuvrability, a speed of 14 knots, are self-righting, and are berthed afloat.

The concentration of controls at the wheelhouse has

The last launch of the Brook (Isle of Wight) lifeboat with horses on Whit Monday, 5 June 1933. The station is now closed

made it possible for the functions of coxswain and mechanic to be combined, and the normal crew to number five instead of seven.

Inshore lifeboats, which are smaller and work only in coastal waters, have a speed of well over 20 knots.

Methods of calling out the crew differ from station to station. At some the telephone is used to call the first man and he fires the maroon to call out the rest of the men. At one station the pressing of a button sets up a loud howling noise and the crew dash to the lifeboat station. A great many other people go too and some of them are used as launchers. The vessel may have to be taken down to the beach in which case a number of planks are laid on the pebbles, or it may be taken by tractor. In earlier days, lifeboats often had to be drawn by horses along rough tracks across country.

While the lifeboat is being launched rockets are fired so that the crew on the vessel may know that help is on the way. The coxswain is in charge of the boat and has the final decision on whether or not it shall be launched if conditions are hazardous. The inshore lifeboat only requires two or three to man it. The motor mechanic is normally the only man who receives a regular salary. The coxswain and other officers are paid a retaining fee. The rest of the crew are paid each time they go to a rescue or spend time exercising. All except the motor mechanic follow their normal occupation during the day, which may be as school teachers, plumbers, farmers, bakers or business men. Many of them are fishermen and all are accustomed to the sea.

Immediately the crew return from a rescue operation they get the boat ready for use again, making sure there are sufficient clothes for a full crew.

Lifeboat societies exist in many parts of the world. An

international conference is held every four years, each time in a different country. The next one, in 1975, will be held in Finland. The Chief Inspector of HM Coastguard attends this conference together with the RNLI delegation.

Like HM Coastguard the RNLI has particularly close ties with the US Coast Guard. Each of the two countries has based some of its motor lifeboats on the other's designs. The RNLI also makes its plans of certain lifeboats available to other European countries and has supervised the building of such.

The RNLI has an active fleet of 138 lifeboats, with a reserve of 30 for relief work. In addition there are 113 inshore lifeboats stationed at different points where need exists. A reserve fleet of 28 of these is maintained. These are housed at the 200 lifeboat stations spaced around the coast of Great Britain.

Lifeboatmen never turn back. As Winston Churchill said when proposing a toast to the Life-boat Institution at its hundredth anniversary dinner: '. . . it drives on with a mercy which does not quail in the presence of death, it drives on as a proof, a symbol, a testimony that man is created in the image of God and that valour and virtue have not perished in the British race'.

Index

94